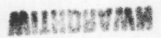

ANIMALS OF THE BIBLE

Animals of the Bible

Text by **ISAAC ASIMOV**

Illustrated by **HOWARD BERELSON**

Doubleday & Company, Inc., Garden City, New York

Author's Dedication

To my wife Janet, once again

Artist's Dedication

à Suzanne Anny, Mon Petit Chou

Library of Congress Catalog Card Number 77–16893
ISBN 0-385-07195-7 Trade
        0-385-07215-5 Prebound
Text copyright © 1978 by Isaac Asimov
Illustrations copyright © 1978 by Howard Berelson

The Bible is a collection of separate documents which were put down in writing at different times.

Some include age-old legends that weren't reduced to writing till after they had been told from memory for centuries. Some are the writings of prophets who preached as long ago as 750 B.C. or as recently as A.D. 100.

For the most part, the documents of the Old Testament deal with the history of the people of Israel and Judah. It includes their notions of how the world began, how the nations came to be, and, in particular, of the ancestors, leaders, and kings of the Israelite tribes. It contains the laws that the Israelites believed to have been handed down by God. It contains songs of praise, proverbs, poems, bits of philosophy.

The New Testament deals with Roman times, when the Israelite territory had come to be the Province of Judea. It tells of the coming of Jesus, of his life, his death, and of what happened immediately after his death.

Yet although the Bible deals with so many different things, it doesn't give us total information. It is not a book of natural history, for instance. It doesn't describe in detail the plants and animals of the lands in which the events it deals with took place.

One reason for this is that the biblical writers felt they had a specific task and in the days before printing, the writing and copying of books was very tedious. You didn't dare waste time on nonessentials. For instance, though there are numbers of passages dealing with Egypt, the pyramids are never mentioned.

Then, too, the people who wrote the Bible assumed all the readers would be familiar with the plants and animals of the land, so that descriptions were not needed.

Animals are mentioned, of course. There are wonder-animals such as the talking serpent in the Garden of Eden. There is the ass on which Balaam rode, which resented being beaten unjustly and said so.

In those days certain animals were important possessions. The early Israelites were herdsmen and to be wealthy meant owning many cattle, sheep, goats, and camels. Such animals are frequently mentioned in that connection.

In addition, the Bible includes elaborate instructions as to which animals may be eaten or sacrificed on the altar. It also makes particular mention of some animals which cannot be eaten or sacrificed.

Animals might be mentioned because they serve as lessons to human beings. The ant is mentioned as an example of hard work, for instance.

Yet it isn't as easy as all that. The Old Testament was written in Hebrew and the animals' names are therefore given in Hebrew. But if a Hebrew word was used 2,500 years ago to represent a certain animal, which animal was it? If the name is just mentioned and no description is given, it is sometimes very difficult to guess. Even the Israelis who live in the land now and who speak Hebrew can't always be sure which animal was meant.

For instance, the book of Job talks about a sea animal, the leviathan, and a land animal, the behemoth. From what is said, they seem to be large animals. The usual guess is that leviathan stands for the whale, but in some places the crocodile seems to fit better. Again, the behemoth is often thought to be the hippopotamus, but it might be the elephant.

Of course, if you read the King James Version of the Bible, you will find the names of many animals given in ordinary English. That, however, doesn't necessarily mean that the animals named in English are actually the animals that were originally named in Hebrew. The translators of the King James Version lived nearly four hundred years ago and they knew less about the lands of the Bible than we do today. Some of their guesses about the animals are surely wrong.

The King James Version isn't the only translation of the Bible that is used by English-speaking people. Some animals are identified in one way in one translation and in another way in another translation.

The Bible is such an interesting book, however, that people never grow tired of hearing about it. It seems, therefore, that we ought to risk getting mixed up in some of these difficulties and do a book about the various animals that are (or that might be) mentioned in it.

I have written a few lines about each one, and Mr. Howard Berelson has painted beautiful pictures of them. Perhaps they will make the Bible mean just a little more to you.

ISAAC ASIMOV

ANIMALS OF THE BIBLE

HIPPOPOTAMUS

Hippopotamus is a Greek word meaning "river horse," and this animal is not mentioned by that name in the Bible. Rather, it is called a behemoth, which is a biblical word meaning "great beast." In the Book of Job it is described as the greatest of all beasts, with bones like strong pieces of brass or bars of iron. But even though it was said to be the masterpiece of all God's work, it was forbidden to live in the mountain regions and was sent to the lowlands, where it was to lie under the trees or swim in the brooks and rivers. The hippopotamus is the largest of river beasts, weighing two or three tons, and measuring about thirteen feet in length and five feet in height. At the time of the writing of the Book of Job, it was found chiefly in the Egyptian sections of the Nile River. Today it lives in the swamps, rivers, and lakes of Central Africa. It eats plants, and comes out of the water at night to find food.

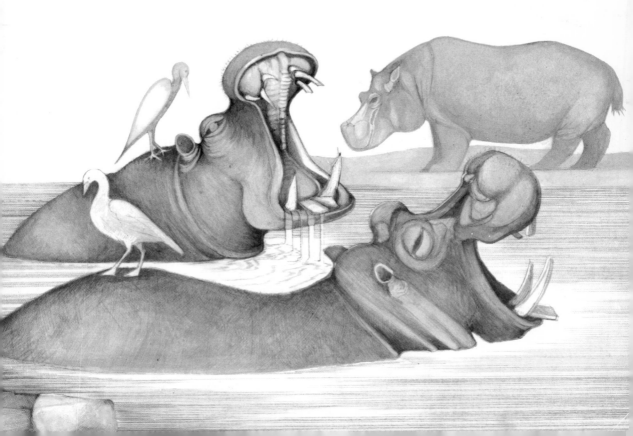

FENNEC

Foxes are among the smaller members of the dog family, and the fennec is a small variety of fox that looks like a cat with long ears. A desert dweller, the fennec stays in its burrow until night, when it hunts. Matthew writes of an observation by Jesus that foxes have holes but He had nowhere to sleep.

LEOPARD

The leopard is one of the large cats and can weigh up to two hundred pounds. It is most noted for its beautiful spotted fur. Jeremiah, skeptical over whether evil men could change their habits, asked ironically whether the leopard could change its spots. The leopard was greatly feared as a predator, and was noted for its stealth and cunning. Isaiah predicted, however, that someday, when evil is finally defeated, the leopard shall lie down with the kid.

ONAGER

The onager, or wild ass, was often hunted and much prized as a beast of burden by its captors. Its instinct for escape was to run toward the open plains. After being hunted for more than two thousand years, it is, today, on the endangered species list. The onager is mentioned several times in the poetical and prophetic books, where it is usually spoken of as being untamable. In the Book of Jeremiah, Jehovah calls Judah "a wild ass used to the wilderness, that snuffeth up the wind at her pleasure."

CAMEL

Two kinds of camels were to be found in the lands of the Bible—the Bactrian camel, with two humps, and the larger, one-humped dromedary. These camels are adapted to desert life and can go for long periods without water, so that they are used in desert-crossing caravans. In Genesis, Abraham's servant rode a camel to Mesopotamia, Jacob's family rode camels when they left Mesopotamia, and Joseph was sold to a group of Ishmaelites who were riding in a camel caravan. Jeremiah refers to a switly running dromedary.

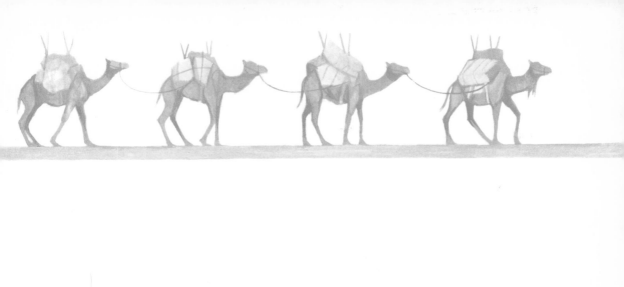

SWINE

Domestic pigs have been kept by herdsmen and farmers for more than two thousand years. Even so, their meat is forbidden to the people of several religions. In Leviticus, God warns Moses that the pig is unclean and must not be eaten or even touched. A pig on a farm, when enraged, can be a very dangerous animal. Matthew tells that Jesus warned us that swine can turn on us and tear us to pieces.

WILD BOAR

The boar is the male pig and the wild boar, the ancestor of our domestic pig, is a fierce and dangerous beast. It was, and is, often hunted partly for sport and partly because a boar at large is dangerous to man and his herds and crops. In the Bible it is mentioned only once. In Psalms we are told that Israel has been ravaged as if a boar out of the wood had wasted it. This is accurate, since a small group of these animals can destroy a whole vineyard in one night.

NUBIAN WILD ASS

The Nubian wild ass is native to Northern Africa, especially around the Egyptian area. This animal is probably the ancestor of our own domestic ass, or donkey, which was tamed more than five thousand years ago. It is a skittish animal that avoids humans. Hosea comments on the solitary habits of the Nubian wild ass when he compares it to the Israelites who had gone into exile like "a wild ass alone by himself."

DONKEY

The donkey, or ass, was probably the first animal used by man (as long ago as 3000 B.C.) to carry burdens and to pull carts. The Bible describes Balaam, in the Book of Numbers, riding his ass to Moab, where he planned to cast evil spells on the Israelites. An angel, visible to the ass only, barred his way. When the ass stopped, Balaam beat it. The ass spoke and complained of the beating. This is the only talking animal in the Bible except for the serpent in the Garden of Eden.

BADGER

The badger is a heavyset member of the weasel family with powerful claws and jaws. It is a savage fighter and is hunted for its skin. The Bible uses the word *takhash* to identify a kind of skin to be brought by the Israelites as one of the materials for building the tabernacle in the Book of Exodus, and this word is translated as badger in the King James Version.

HYENA

The striped hyena is a member of the dog family possessing a powerful body and very strong jaws. This scavenger was common in ancient Egypt. Until this century, no English translations of the Bible contained a mention of this animal. But now some scholars, in translating the First Book of Samuel, tell of a raiding party going to the Valley of the Hyenas.

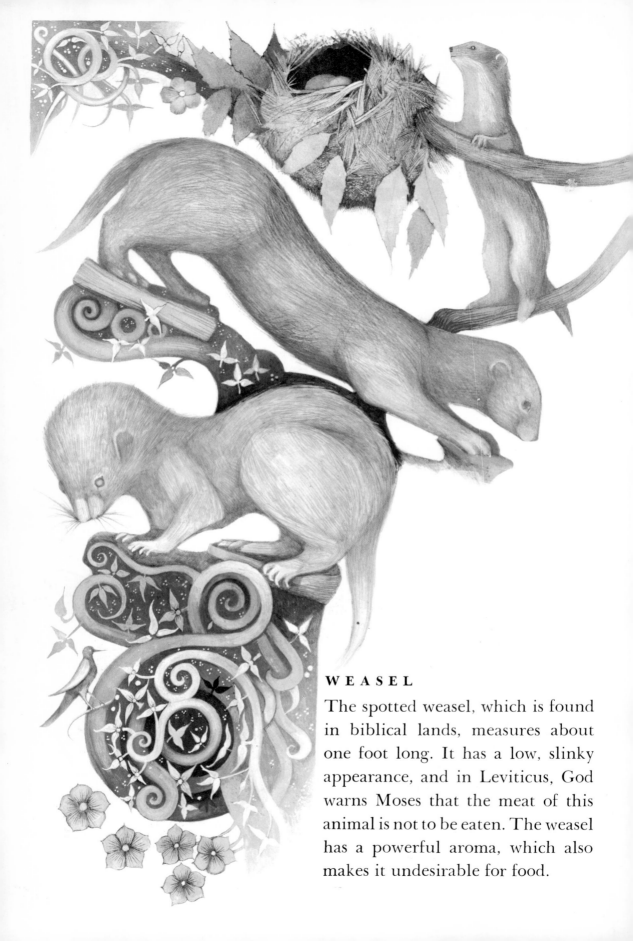

WEASEL

The spotted weasel, which is found in biblical lands, measures about one foot long. It has a low, slinky appearance, and in Leviticus, God warns Moses that the meat of this animal is not to be eaten. The weasel has a powerful aroma, which also makes it undesirable for food.

PORCUPINE

The crested porcupine is the largest rodent in the biblical region. It is a solitary animal living in burrows and possessing pointed quills which will stick in attacking animals. In some translations of Isaiah, God threatens to turn cities into mere homes for porcupines.

JACKAL

The jackal is one of the smaller members of the dog family. It hunts by night and avoids the haunts of man. The jackal makes a sad yelping sound in the evenings. In many translations of the Bible, Isaiah predicts that Babylon will be so destroyed that jackals will be crying in its desolate ruins.

DESERT FOX

The desert fox can be found in the
drier parts of Israel and Egypt. It is
rather similar to the European red
fox in appearance, but it is not a
woodland animal. In Lamentations it
is said that foxes roamed on Mount
Zion because it was so desolate.
However, many translators believe
that the passage refers to jackals.

AUROCHS

The aurochs is the ancestor of our modern domestic cattle. It is now extinct, but existed as late as the 1600s. This wild ox was a strong and dangerous animal. In modern translations of the Psalms, God is asked to save us from the horns of the wild oxen.

CATTLE

The expression "cattle" can sometimes be used to describe all domestic animals, but usually it means bulls and cows, oxen and calves. To herdsmen of biblical times, the animals they owned were the chief way of counting wealth. Thus, when Abram left Egypt, as described in Genesis, he was very rich in cattle, in silver, and in gold.

CATS

Domestic cats were raised by the ancient Egyptians and Babylonians to keep mice and other rodents out of the royal granaries. They were also kept in their holy temples. The Egyptians also worshiped the cat and made statues of the animal. In Baruch, Jeremiah comforts those who are about to become Babylonian slaves, by pointing out that there are cats in the temples of that country, so their gods must be false. The cheetah is one of the large members of the cat family. Because it is the fastest land animal, the Egyptians used it for hunting game. In Habakkuk we are told that the Chaldeans had horses that were swifter than leopards. Here the hunting leopard, or cheetah, is probably what is meant.

HORSE

The horse was tamed about 2000 B.C. The Asian nomads used horses to conquer Babylonia and Egypt. The Egyptians, as described in Exodus, pursued the Israelites with horse and chariot.

MULE

The mule is the offspring of a female horse and a male donkey. In the time of David, mules were used by members of the royal house. When David was dying, as described in the First Book of Kings, he showed his desire to have Solomon succeed him by directing Solomon to ride on his mule.

MONKEYS

There are no apes or monkeys native to the lands of the Bible. But some had been imported from India, Ceylon, and the more southern regions of Africa. Very common were the rhesus monkey and the type of baboon which the Egyptians trained. In the First Book of the Kings, we are told that so great was the power and wealth of King Solomon that his navies brought in exotic goods from distant regions, including apes and baboons.

IBEX

The ibex is a wild goat living in mountainous areas and other rocky places, and may be what is meant by the biblical word *yael*. In the First Book of Samuel, David, in his flight from Saul, is described as hiding among the rocks of the wild goats.

GOAT

The goat was among the first animals to be domesticated by man as a source of food and milk. However, it was too small to be of use as a work animal. The herds of rich men usually included many goats. The First Book of Samuel mentions Nabal, who lived at Mount Carmel in David's time and owned a thousand goats. Sometimes the Bible contrasts goats with the more peaceful sheep, making them symbolize sinners.

MOUSE

The Hebrew word *akhbar,* translated as mouse in the King James Version of the Bible, is a general term covering all the small rodents of the rat and mouse family. *Akhbar* literally means "destruction of grain." In the First Book of Samuel we are told that the Philistines had to offer up five golden mice as a guilt offering to end a disease plague. Some scholars think that this indicates that the people of biblical times may have understood that rodents spread disease.

HARE

The hare is mentioned only twice in the Bible, in Leviticus and in Deuteronomy. In each case, it is listed as an animal that is not to be eaten, because it does not have a cloven foot and yet chews a cud. Actually, the hare does not chew a cud, but it does look as though it does. This is because of the restless motion of nose and lips as it sniffs at the air for possible signs of danger.

SHEEP

Sheep, including ewes, lambs, and rams, are mentioned 742 times in the Bible, perhaps because they made up the largest part of the herds of the patriarchs. In the Book of Genesis, when Jacob and his sons came to Egypt and were asked their occupation by the Pharaoh, they answered, "Thy servants are shepherds, both we, and also our fathers." The need to care for the sheep, which supplied meat, milk, and wool, made it common to describe kings, and even God, as shepherds guarding a flock.

AOUDAD

The aoudad, or Barbary sheep, is an animal native to North Africa. In Deuteronomy it is listed as one of the animals that can be eaten by man. In the King James Version it is called the chamois, but that is probably a mistranslation, since the chamois is a mountain goat found in Europe and not in biblical lands.

ELEPHANT

There are two species of elephants, the Indian and the African. This animal was imported to the biblical lands after Alexander the Great encountered them being used in warfare by the soldiers of India in 326 B.C. For a couple of centuries thereafter, various armies in the Mediterranean area used elephants. War elephants are mentioned several times in the Books of the Maccabees, which deal with the Judean rebellion against the Syrians in 168 B.C. There are also nine references to ivory in the Bible.

ADDAX

The addax is a heavyset antelope that is native to North Africa. It has broad hooves, like a camel, which enable it to travel in loose sand. It also has twisted horns, and its belly is white. This animal, called the pygarg or the ibex in some translations, is mentioned in Deuteronomy as one that can be eaten by man.

HARTEBEEST

The hartebeest is an antelope with a long face and horns that spread apart and sweep back. They are most common in South Africa, but one species, the bubal, is native to North Africa. The bubal may be what is meant by the biblical word *yahmur*, which is mentioned in Deuteronomy among the animals that men are permitted to eat.

FALLOW DEER

The fallow deer is a medium-sized member of the deer family, standing about three feet high, and is native to the Mediterranean area and western Asia. In the First Book of Kings, it is listed as one of the animals that was eaten at the court of King Solomon.

ROE DEER

The roe deer is smaller than the red deer or the fallow deer. It has short antlers, almost no tail, and lives in small family groups. It usually stays in the woods and comes out only to graze in the open fields. Some people can be described, as they are in the Second Book of Samuel, as being "as light of foot as a wild roe."

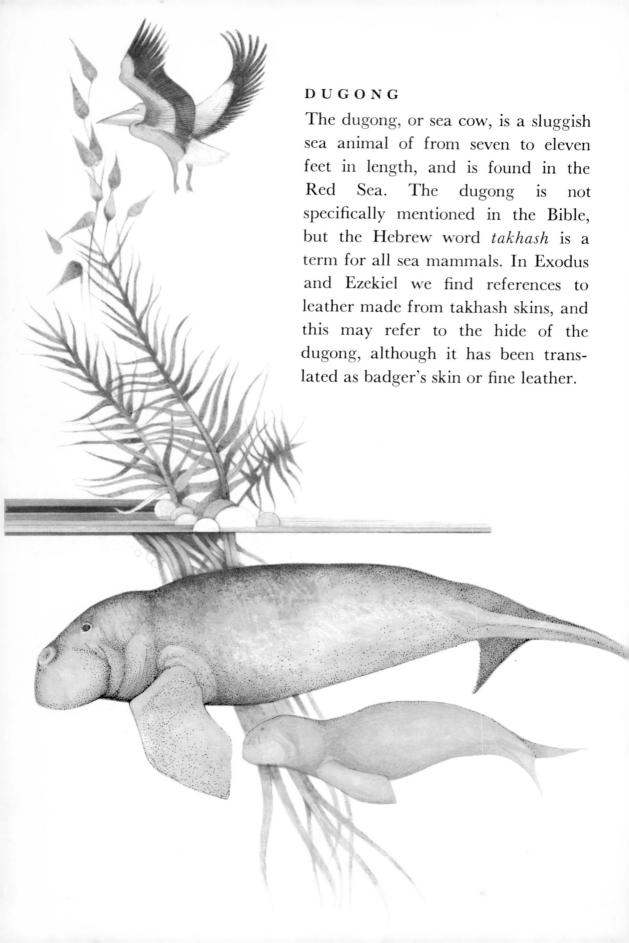

DUGONG

The dugong, or sea cow, is a sluggish sea animal of from seven to eleven feet in length, and is found in the Red Sea. The dugong is not specifically mentioned in the Bible, but the Hebrew word *takhash* is a term for all sea mammals. In Exodus and Ezekiel we find references to leather made from takhash skins, and this may refer to the hide of the dugong, although it has been translated as badger's skin or fine leather.

HYRAX

The hyrax is a small rodentlike animal with little hooves on the first and third toe of the hind leg and a claw on the second toe. In the King James Version, it is referred to as a "coney." In Proverbs it is said that the coneys are but feeble folk, yet they make their houses in the rocks.

GAZELLE

The gazelle belongs to the antelope family, some of which live in the biblical lands. It is a small animal, some three feet high, with graceful curved horns, and is noted for its speed. It was also prized for its meat, and traps were set for it. In Ecclesiasticus it is said, "He has fled like a gazelle from the snare."

RED DEER

The biblical word *ayyal* may refer to deer generally. The male red deer is known as the hart or the stag, and the female is called the hind. In the Song of Songs the bride compares her beloved to a young stag, leaping and bounding over the hills.

RED FOX

The red fox is the only member of the dog family to have survived in large numbers in the European wild. It is also found in North America, Asia, India, and Africa north of the Sahara. It lives in the more wooded areas, and is probably the animal in the Song of Songs —the little foxes that spoil the vines.

BEAR

The Syrian bear roamed the biblical lands in Old Testament times, though there are none there today. In the First Book of Samuel, David told King Saul how he had rescued the sheep he guarded from lions and bears. In the Second Book of Kings, when the prophet Elisha was mocked by children, she-bears came from the wood and attacked them.

ORYX

The oryx is an antelope, once plentiful throughout Palestine, Arabia, and Iraq. In the Book of Isaiah, God speaks to the people of Jerusalem and says, according to a modern translation, "Your sons lie helpless like an antelope trapped in a net." The oryx is probably the antelope that is meant. Both male and female oryxes have two long, sharp-edged horns that are straight or slightly curved. Seen from the side, one horn hides the other. Although the unicorn of the Bible is an imaginary animal, the notion of an animal like a horse with one, long, straight horn on its forehead may have arisen from the appearance of the oryx. In Deuteronomy, some translations tell of Moses describing Joseph: "His horns are like the horns of unicorns."

WOLF

The wolf of the biblical lands was not as large and as fearsome as the wolves of more northerly regions. Still, it could be used as a symbol of danger and injustice. In Zephaniah unjust judges are compared to wolves. And in the Gospel According to Saint Matthew, when Jesus sent his apostles out into the land to preach the gospel, he said, "I send you forth as sheep in the midst of wolves."

DOG

The dog was not a family pet in biblical times. It was a scavenger and so was given scraps to eat, as was ordered in Exodus. To use the word "dog" to describe a person was insulting. In the First Book of Samuel, when David approached Goliath with only his staff and a sling, Goliath said, "Am I a dog, that thou comest to me with staves?"

LION

The lion was common in biblical lands, although it is now not found there. It was a smaller variety than the great African lion, but it was used as a symbol of valor, strength, and danger. In the Book of Judges, it is a sign of the superhuman strength of Samson that he killed a lion with his bare hands. In the Book of Isaiah, we are told that in the final age things will be so peaceful that the lion will eat straw like the ox.

MOLE RAT

Moles are small burrowing animals that live on worms and insects and have feeble vision or none at all; but they are not found in the lands of the Bible. But there is a mole rat there —a rodent that leads a similar life and looks like the mole. When Isaiah predicts that men will throw their false idols to the moles, he was probably referring to the mole rats.

BAT

Bats are the only flying mammals. They have hair and give birth to living young, which they suckle with mother's milk. In Leviticus, however, the bat, because it can fly, is listed among the birds that should not be eaten.

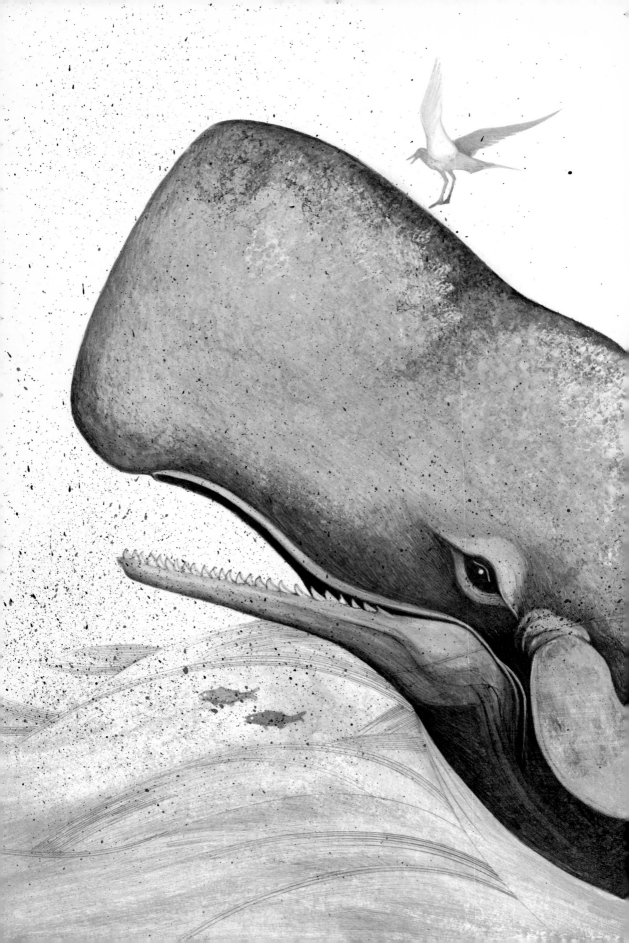

WHALE

The biblical word *tannin* means a large sea monster, and, in the King James Version, is translated as whale. In Genesis the first living things created by God were great whales. The Book of Jonah tells of Jonah being swallowed by a great fish and staying inside that fish for three days and three nights. The story of Jonah in the whale is referred to in the Gospel According to Saint Matthew.

Widely known for both his science fiction and his serious scientific essays, ISAAC ASIMOV has written more than 190 books on subjects ranging from physics to mythology, from mathematics to the Bible. Born in Russia in 1920, Dr. Asimov came to Brooklyn with his family at the age of three, received his Ph.D. from Columbia University in 1948, and in the following year joined the faculty of Boston University School of Medicine. He has written many stories about the Bible, including his best-selling *The Story of Ruth*. He lives in New York City.

HOWARD BERELSON is a graduate of Pratt Institute, where he studied industrial design and sculpture. Since that time, he has worked at various posts teaching art and sculpture. A recent trip to northern France, with its medieval tapestries and stained glass, provided a rich source of imagery for the feeling of this book. *Chess for Children and the Young at Heart* and *The Office Gardener* are books that Mr. Berelson has recently illustrated.